MAGICICADA

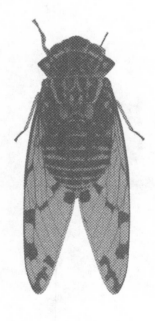

MAGICICADA
& other marvels

poems by
Kathleen Brewin Lewis

SHANTI ARTS PUBLISHING
BRUNSWICK, MAINE

MAGICICADA
& other marvels

Published by Shanti Arts Publishing
Designed by Shanti Arts Designs

Cover image and image on half-title page by
Rosalee Lewis and used with her permission.

Shanti Arts LLC
193 Hillside Road
Brunswick, Maine 04011
shantiarts.com

Printed in the United States of America

ISBN: 978-1-956056-55-6 (softcover)

Library of Congress Control Number: 2022943697

for my marvelous family

Contents

Autobiography ❧

Your first knowledge, the nooks and crannies
of your parents' bodies: crooks of their arms,
scent of their necks, your head resting
between their breasts and collarbones.

Your first loves, the small, soft things—
feathers, young animals, blushing puffs of bloom
from the mimosa tree. Start to collect
the harder things: stones, sticks, shells—
pockets and pails of them. Treasures.

Become graceful. Enter the water,
begin to swim. Dance unashamed, arms wide.
Legs pump the creaking swing,
arc against the sky.

Learn to pay your respects: climb trees,
discover, but do not touch, birds' nests.
Study the contents of the tidal pool—
sand dollar, sea olive, translucent crab.
Smell the iris; do not pick it.
Resolve to break nothing.

July's Thick Kingdom 🦅

Chalice of cherries,
bloody juice on the chin.
A sorcerer's crumbling of mint.
The brown hare spent
and snagged in the bramble,
the huntsman's lost arrow bent.
Crown of clouds, throne of honeysuckle,
flask of dandelion wine. The falcon
alights on a gauntlet of broom moss.
Sunset flares through the regal pines.

In the dwindling glow, fireflies.
In the raptor's beak, a golden coin.

Magicicada 🐞

Magicicada is the genus of the periodical cicadas of eastern North America. A brood spends seventeen years underground before emerging en masse.

Three cicadas left their husks
on the underside of a linden branch,
as if The Rapture had occurred.
The bigger mystery
is what the insects had been doing
underground for 17 years
before they climbed out of the earth
to mate and die.

Once my young hound swallowed one
and ran to me, buzzing and screeching
as if possessed. I pried her muzzle open
and pulled the crunchy creature
from her throat. It scolded us
as it took flight.

The afternoon is warm. I hear
the brood juddering in the yard.
I try to remember where I was
when the cicadas were here before,
ponder where I might be 17 years hence.
Raising children, grieving my father
the last time; on my way
to becoming a husk the next.
Time—raucous, relentless—flies.

Peaceful, In Spite of It All 🖎

*In 1864, four thousand Union and Confederate soldiers
died in the Battle of Kennesaw Mountain.*

*In 1982, the City Council of Kennesaw passed an ordinance
requiring the head of every household to own a gun,
with ammunition.*

On the long, slim path through the meadow at Kennesaw
Mountain Battlefield: cricket chorus, white butterflies. I'm
somewhere out of time. I've never seen ghost soldiers there,
but I've sensed their gun-smoked presence. I wonder if the
ghost-men notice me, strolling across this place, growing
older by the minute, at ease.

In the town of Kennesaw: growling pick-up trucks stickered
with Stars and Bars. Big Pie in the Sky Pizza advertises
slices *big as your head*. There's a voracious appetite for the
Second Amendment there. Some wars, it seems, are still
being fought.

Today I've come to hike the mountain. The climb yields
titanic views of battlefield and town. Atlanta office towers
shimmer, distant. Deer, accustomed to visitors, forage
within a few feet of the trail. Heads lowered, legs slender as
cello bows, they turn their soft beige backs to me, innocent,
unafraid.

The Shoal Lilies

It's not what you were expecting
as you kayaked around the bend,
it's what you received:
throngs of tall white lilies—
rare six-pointed stars—
thriving on the shoals.
Blooming islands rooted
in the crevices between
the river rocks, scenting the air.
You found a watery path
through a stand of them,
lifted your paddle, let the current
pull you along. Your heart,
tugged and tattered,
swung open and let
a vagrant peace flow in.
That such abundance
was here in the world
and you hadn't known it existed
until this day. This day,
the day of the shoal lilies
along the Broad River.

There Are Days ✒

you scrounge the last onion
from the dry field,
bruise a heel
on some stone from the river,
rake a serrated elm leaf
across your blue wrist.
This is not one of those days.

This is a day
you lace your fingers
into thick grass,
rouse yourself
with a sense of belonging,
tread so lightly on sandy soil,
you leave a tender imprint.

Dovetail these:
sprout of radish
call of nuthatch,
flight of dragonfly,
whiff of rain. Snap
a forked branch
from the hazel tree;
divine the source
of this day.

Childhood, Heavy with Hydrangea 🦢

Voluptuous mopheads—
pink, blue, purple—
mob summer's yard.

On a card table
your mother has arranged
some clipped blues
with fern, phlox,
and bellflower,
in a white pitcher.

Your father
grills hamburgers
while you play tag
with the neighbors.

Sundown.
Grown-ups talk
and children lie
on quilts in grass,
pretending not to listen.
The dog curls beside you.
Out the corner of your eye,
glint of firefly.

Your mother. Your father.
That fragrant life.

The Largesse of Morning 🕊

Wake up slender
to faint light
seeping through shutters.

The sun, a freshly peeled orange,
begins its climb;
dawn spreads out a picnic
on bright cloth.

Breakfast on melon, egg, hope—
grant yourself
reprieve from disbelieving.
Breathe the aroma
of exonerated earth.

The day is bound to narrow,
its conclusion
promises to be dark.
For now the world
is filling with radiance.
See how the morning glories
trumpet on the white fence.

Voracity

I want to know
the common names
of growing things—
ferns, oaks, sumac,
then I want to break
into their hearts,
slit their stems
with my thumbnail,
peel bark, splinter twigs,
place spores, pollen, pith, phloem
on my tongue's tip,
swallow sap. Crack
the botanic bones
of this evergreen world,
pry ripe marrow—
and I will
renounce the trail,
go deeper into woods,
stand in thick rain to do it.

Petrichor

Two geologists made this word
from the Greek, *petros* for stone,
and *ichor*, for the liquid that flows
through the veins of the gods.
They wanted to name the scent
of parched earth after fresh rain:
The reconstituted redolence
of salted silt marbled
with terracotta.
This old, dry world
brought back to loamy life.

Another word for *mercy*.

Bliss

I'm not exactly certain
what circadian rhythms are,
not really sure I want to know,
content to love the sound of them,
imagine what they might be:
Celadon moth circling
rusty porch light, pair of mallards
asleep on black pond, ocean's
swell and sweep of shore,
the crash diets of the moon.

A dictionary could end
the mystery, lift the veil
separating fantasy from fact.

I would rather
keep picturing:
a striped feather
scything the air,
graceful dance
between man and beast,
the planets afloat
in a susurrant place,
honeybees droning
deep
in bright
blossoms.

Eggshell

Morning is a chiffon scarf. A child
steps out into soft light,
a spotted egg cupped in his hands.
I rest my palm on the place where
his bowed head meets his slim neck.
Sometimes this is prophecy,
sometimes recollection.
To touch him this way is always a blessing.

Afternoon, a chambray shirt, rolls its sleeves up.
The boy lifts his head, tells me
of his dreaming, turns his attention
to the plunge of a red-tailed hawk.
There is composure in his turning.
His shoulders broaden, he grows taller than I.
The egg cracks open. The night
is a woolen coat with silver buttons.

Whereupon the Writer Thinks She Is the Center of the Universe 🖋

In a lonely corner of the night,
she sits writing at the kitchen table
while her house sleeps. The outside
is trying to come in.

Dusty moths and brown beetles
are beating on the glass,
covering the windowpanes
with their soft wings and crisp bodies,
drawn to, absolutely craving,
her light.

She is spooked, distracted,
she is finally flattered,
writing more intently
for her fluttering audience,
moved by the staccato
of their gentle collisions.

This night is alive, she is thinking,
it is pulsing with the beat of my heart.
And all eyes—
all of the tiny, glittering eyes—
are on me.

A Story of the Earth 🐦

In the great green eye of the world,
floats the smallest bird, the tallest bear.

You, me, our children singing
like aspen leaves.

And the old and broken
are borne aloft—as leaping mackerel,
luna moths, cicadas drinking
in sap-thick trees.

Dripping honeycomb,
foaming waterfall,
nestled clutch of eggs.

This earth is succulent, I tell you.

Rain patters its testimony
into forgiving sand.

Trespass 🖋

On the trail to the ruined textile mill, the wild azaleas
are in bloom, the magnolia thick with fat white buds.

I mean to set my mantle of care down beside
this stony creek, hide it among the hardwoods.

Each step is a lightening, the sound of water
flowing over rocks a mercy.

After a mile or more, I reach the Civil War relic,
banked and boarded beside the shoals.

There's a breach in the old bricks and I step through,
into the dim and dusty quiet.

A rustling in the eaves, small shower of leaves.
Doves or pigeons, I imagine, a snug nest of squirrels.

Instead a length of black rope falls from the rafters,
thuds on the ground, slithers into a dark corner.

I shiver, slip back where I came from—
into the day, this spring, this world.

Invasive Species 🕊

A thin stream lies
at the bottom of the hill
in the woods
behind our house. Once
the children and I
hiked down in rainboots,
in case copperheads coiled
in the thick ivy. English ivy,
planted by suburban landscapers
in the 1960s. It escaped the yard.

The stream glittered
with mica flecks and fool's gold,
bits of broken glass.
Coyote paw prints pocked
the wet sand, and there were
scores of tiny snail shells
strewn along the water line.
We discovered an old beekeeping box,
possible arrowhead, belt of barbed wire
embedded in a long-standing oak.

*Don't ever come down here
without me*, I told the kids,
now that they knew the way.
We never went back.
We left the woods, the hill, the stream
to the clutches of the ivy.

By June the Light Begins to Breathe 🖎

spring rains
have cleared the air
and the year is sure of itself,
at ease. Corn blades up
through warmed soil.
Tomatoes fatten. Trees
hide children in their leafy arms.
The sky is its usual blue,
ordinary, extraordinary,
quotidian, dear. The bright
hemisphere draws in, blows out,
like the respiration
of saffron-robed monks.

The Husker 🖋

She's an insatiable shucker, pulling back
the stiff green leaves, listening hungrily
to the rasp and rip. She consumes herself
with the stripping, snaps off the stump, plucks
each clingy strand of the tassel. Then she rubs
her index finger over the rows of bulging kernels
as if they were braille or pearls or little teeth,
piles the yellow spikes tenderly
into the crisper of her fridge.

To justify her habit, she prepares fresh corn salads
with red onion, cider vinegar, torn basil,
a little salt, or sautés the bright kernels in olive oil
with shrimp and diced tomatoes. Her husband sighs
at the frequency of these dishes. When they make love,
she conjures the sound of the husking,
strokes her cheek with a lock of corn silk
after he rolls over, falls asleep.

She dreams of walking
through acres of summer cornfields,
tables loaded with brimming bushels
just waiting for her touch.
All that tightly guarded ripeness!
The saddest thing she can think of
is the colorless silence of the gnawed cob.

Parched

Midsummer day,
blazing, breathless.
The sky throws down
a handful of rain
and the grass
gets its hopes up.
It doesn't want to wither,
any more than you or I.

Sapelo 🌊

*In the 1850s, 385 slaves lived and toiled
on this Georgia barrier island.*

This sultry place, built
on the bare backs of slaves:
malarial rice fields, shell-studded
tabby structures, cane and cotton
plantations, solitary lighthouse. All

ruins now, but for the lighthouse—
rebuilt, relit, in a better century.
A ninth generation ferries the sound
to weekday work on the mainland,
digs Saturday clams and oysters
from deep mud at low tide. Still

the island mourns.
Its twisted oaks wear
shrouds of Spanish moss,
bear boughs heavy
with resurrection fern. Thick

rattlesnakes drape and sun
on the planter's headstone.

Above All Else 🦅

The meadow, falling into shade.
A worn path through oat grass,
thistle, milkweed. This lofty view
from the outcrop: cursive river,
written in graphite. In the draft
of late afternoon, buzzards soar
with such grace, I nearly forget
why they're here.

Fluent in Rivers

Before you knew me,
before I came to root myself
in these red clay hills beside your father,
I lived by the coastline,
         swam its creeks and rivers.

Afloat in brackishness,
watching blue crabs pedal
sideways and away,
I heard the cry of the marsh hen,
         was solitary but never afraid.

Shoulders draped with dark water,
I let cool tendrils of current
carry me around the bend,
until I turned, kicked, stroked my way back
         to the sunburnt dock, the anchor of its ladder.

The clacking of grizzled oyster beds,
white heron lifting over green marsh,
fish leaping like celebrants,
the suck, seep of tidal life,
         holding my breath, gliding through all.

Today the wind moans around the house,
rattles the cellar door. I peel potatoes
while you sleep in the back bedroom.
When you wake, I need to tell you:
         Before you knew me,
         before I was your mother,
         I swam through summer,
         was fluent in rivers.

The Emissaries 🐟

Roasted oysters have been palmed, shucked, the party moved indoors. Light, laughter spill onto the blackened bluff. I've walked down to the river. At the sound of my footsteps on the empty dock, a great blue heron lifts, flaps into darkness.

I hear them before I see them—a pair of dolphins announcing their presence with bursts of their blowholes. In the moonlight on the gray water, they disappear, reappear, arcing their bodies so perfectly, they seem to be circular. I take my hands out of my coat pockets, unhunch my shoulders. The dolphins turn, fin out of sight, their chuffs growing fainter as they move up the deep and stone-cold river.

Lowcountry River ✐

There is no turning back, only turning.

Slim girl on floating dock, head bent over crab line.
Hand over hand, she pulls the line nimbly between thumb
and forefinger, tricking the crab out of the river and into the net.

The girl becomes a woman who breaks
her mother's heart. Has a daughter who will break
her heart, has a granddaughter.
All of them will turn into old women.

The river bends out of sight, sends its creeky fingers into the marsh.

You and me,
and all the grand, small things
that hardly mattered, and meant the world.

The water teems with silversides, brown shrimp, blue crab.

Distant Shore 🖋

Thank you, Mama

You're only a foot or so from being able to touch bottom—
salty waves bobbling you—but your mother thinks
you're out too far. She stands at water's edge
beckoning. You were just loosening, starting to feel
sleek and untethered, and you aren't ready
to give up these sensations, head to shore, sit and build
another drip castle. You shake her off, but now
she wades knee-high into the ocean calling your name.
The beach-bent waves slap her chest,
and you can't have that, so you stroke in
to the crowded shallows, petulance dripping
from your scrawny shoulders.

And then you're standing at the window
of your big-city apartment trying to decide
whether to head out to the bars again.
The night is cold. You look out at a sea of lights
that shine for no one in particular.
It is then you will recall your mother
standing on the shore, slim and vigilant
in a bright bathing suit. You will remember the way
the ocean lifted you, then let you down.
Your toes brushed the sand, the undertow
tugged at your feet, but you kicked it away.

Your mother has raised her arm,
she beckons to you.
She's trying to tell you
you're out too far.

Old Beach House 🕊

for Rosalee

We rented my family's old beach house last October, the one
my father sold fifteen years ago when we learned his cancer
had spread. The white clapboard house was nicer than it
used to be, with a new bathroom and better kitchen, but
the dark paneled walls were still warm and rich, the front
windows framed the same Back River sunset. I could swear
I saw my little girl climb out of the bathtub and toddle into
the bedroom, her head ringed in wet curls, baby bottom
bare and round, little feet slapping the wood floor. But when
I followed her into the room, there was just a young woman
standing there in jeans and a soft sweater, brushing her
long blonde hair in front of the mirror.

Sleepwalking on a Summer Night 🦢

What roused you—just enough to set your limbs in motion,
carry you to the backyard where the moon was waning?
A place of dissolution, as the garden was spent from days of heat.
Only the rosemary remained.

You tread softly in your white nightgown, sliding
the door open as if it were a fragile portal, your life a secret.
Sat flat-eyed, cross-legged on the brittle grass.
Effigy of your sentient self.

Fingertips pressed together, not quite in prayer,
for it was still too hot to be holy. Bats flitted like swallows
over your head in the endangered moonlight
When will it rain?

You finally rose, returned to your lavender linen,
woke at first light, puzzled: *Why a stone in your hand,
dried leaf in your hair?* Hair dark as bat wings,
hand as pale as the moon.

Waxing Poetic 🖋

If you can cup the moon in your right hand, it's waxing.
If you can cup it in your left, it's waning.

The moon is just past full, my love,
less a sliver on the right,
and I have much to say to you
before the rend of night,
before pronouncing denouement
on something rare and fine,
in deference to indifference
without reason, but with rhyme.

I saw you slipping out-of-doors,
your long stride to the left,
and I have gathered you are filled
with something like regret.
Something kin to insouciance
leavened with disdain,
a silent declaration that
our merger's on the wane.

If I danced well, I'd join you
in a dress of silver light,
remind you that we still can be
the darlings of the night,
but I am clumsy with my feet
as well as with my art.
Uncup that cold, inconstant orb;
exchange it for your heart.

The moon is almost full, my love,
just a shaving off the right.

Encounter in a Dry Riverbed 🐦

There are stones here—ivory, gray—
rubbed ovoid and smooth
by a vanished river.
Firs stand silent in pale breeze.

Lone raptor in the sky:
black against blue.
White vapor trail stunning
as a God-made thing.
A riot of wildflowers.

The red fox appears, long legs,
coal stockings. He stops, stares,
passes close enough
to touch. I will never
be the same.

Collusion on the Middle Provo 🐟

He knows it is my first time
so he is patient, leading me
down the path to the riverbed,
through meadows of red clover,
lamb's ears, saffron yarrow.

He stands me amid the stones
in the river's rush, places
the rod in my hand, covers
my hand with his, talks of technique:
how to cast, mend, hook, reel.
And so I unfurl, over and over again,
until I feel what he means:
the tug and tear of a fish on the line.

Let the line run when the fish jerks,
he coaches, *reel it smoothly in as the fish tires.*
And when the trout rises, he laughs,
congratulates me, scoops
my fish into his net,
tells me I'm a natural.

He says to wet my hands
in the bracing current then cup them
while he unhooks, lifts, puts the trout
in touch with me.

I want to press my lips to her,
she is so marvelous, pulsing, sleek
against my palms, instead I bend
and whisper so he can't hear me,
that I'm sorry for hurting her
and I wish her well.

I turn my back to him,
lower her into the glistening river
that snatches, bears her away.

Camellias 🦢

for Lafe

French doors open
onto the hospice courtyard
and from his bed
he points to a camellia bush
heavy with red blossoms.

That's going to be my barometer, he says.
I'll look at it to see which way
the wind's blowing.
I saw those flowers turn their heads
into the sun this morning.
Now they've turned their backs on me.

He watches the bush,
the blossoms, the breeze all day
and then, after supper,
which he does not eat,
he turns his back on the camellias
and they become
the last blooms he ever witnesses.

And So, September 🖤

arrives to straddle the seasons—
parching heat, then spattering rain,
too late to save the corn but in time
to sprout the pumpkin. There will be
plenty of down-to-earth suns to sell
at fall farmers markets, hickory nuts
and collards, cured hams and radishes,
amber jars of honey. Dahlias wrapped
in dampened newsprint; cinnamon-laced pies.
The solstice has been recalled, the equinox
advances. Soon—a heady whiff
of wood smoke. Yellow leaves stunning
the black pond.

Order *Lepidoptera*, Family *Papilionoidea* ⚭

He loves them for their colors, the silence of their flight,
their fragility, which is something like his own.
His room is filled with cases of their splayed beauty.
He's told himself the creatures were found lying
on soft paths at the end of their life cycles.
He can't believe they were caught to be pinned down.

He studies his field guide, strives to learn the Latin:
Vanessa atalanta, Thymelicus silvestris, Inachis io.
He's already memorized the common names
that reflect their hues—Clouded Yellow, Purple Hairstreak,
Mazarine Blue.

Mother is a butterfly, he thinks. She knows how
to touch him lightly in ways he can bear. Sometimes
she tells him she needs to hug him, would he be brave
for a few seconds and let her hold him gently? He would.
Mother smells like lilies. Father shakes his hand too hard.

He's promised to sit at the table, have Thanksgiving dinner
with the family, *try very, very hard* to make conversation
with his cousins. *Earth to Jonathan!* his little brother trumpets,
when he doesn't realize Aunt Beryl is trying to pass him
the sweet potatoes. Everyone together is so noisy.
Sister lays two fingers on his knee, which calms him.
He wonders if she is training to be a mother.

He answers a question from his uncle, remembers
to make eye contact, eats the food on his plate
in his usual clockwise fashion. Then he notices the centerpiece,
a hollowed-out pumpkin filled with flowers, thinks
how the mums are the color of the Sooty Copper,
has to excuse himself from the table, return to his room
full of bright and delicate wings.

On the Chestatee, Late September 🐚

The river runs crooked,
chattering, cold—
nudging the trout redds.
Armored turtles
assemble on black logs,
drench in sunlight.
The gray fox drinks.
In trees, gauzy
sacks of webworm
dissolve into clouds
of white moths.
A hawk screams
as it dives.

Luna Moth 🪶

She has one week to live.

The first night, she appears
at my window: finch-sized,
owl-spotted, swallow-tailed.
Astounding me with her
vivid green beauty.

Mouthless, she is not driven
by ordinary hunger. She craves
moonlight and streetlight, mates
after midnight, leaves legions
of eggs on the underside of
black walnut leaves.

Her caterpillar offspring
will never know her.
After the seventh day, I find her
in the grass, lime wings
faded to celadon and tattering
in the wind.

Raven, in the Back of Beyond 🖋

Black bird shines
in the morning sun,
strutting the lawn,
gifting you a dark feather.
Speak to him,
he cocks his head, knows
what you do not know,
forgives you. With a caw
and two wingbeats,
he lifts, leaves you
yearning to be
nothing more
than three pounds
of iridescent ebony
trapezing the sky,
vanishing in
to the back of beyond.

Coyote ❧

There you are, standing by my swimming pool.
I've never seen you before, but I know who you are.
You're more handsome than I've been led to believe.
Your presence explains the missing cat signs
around the neighborhood, why I never see
brown bunnies on the lawn anymore.
And all the while I've been watching you,
you've never taken your golden eyes
off me. I am the one who finally looks away.

The Last Wild Passenger Pigeon Makes Her Concession Speech 🖋

My mother called me *Piqua*, as she bent
over our warm whorl with bits of worm.

A word she taught me: *flock*.
How I dreamt of them, a feathered rising
above the trees, cries of *coo-roo too-coo*.
Such safety in numbers, winged joy!

They hunted us, devoured us.
One day we were gone. I combed
the woods for markings like mine:
blue-gray head, rosy breast, graceful neck.
I cooed and clucked into the deep hush.

I have lost the race.

Change of Heart 🐾

On the interstate, I make eye contact with a black cow
being pulled past my window in a muddy trailer. She stands
slew-footed to keep from losing balance on the cold metal.
Her eye is a fringed pond, dark and deep. I blink, picture
her grazing in a bright field. Now she's on the road to ruin,
white card hanging from a punctured ear, rag-tag jewelry.
Maybe she isn't self-aware, doesn't care, thinks she's just
along for the ride. When I get home, I unpack my groceries,
put the flank steak I just purchased in the farthest reaches
of the freezer.

The (Barely) Bearable Heaviness of Being—Fall 2017 🕿

with apologies to Milan Kundera

We sit on the front porch
listening to leaves fall,
she in her fleece bathrobe,
I in my quilted coat. The cat deposits
a limp sparrow at my feet.

The first frost has crept in
during the night
and killed the coleus,
robbing us of fuchsia
and lime green,
leaving us brown.

To the west,
houses and forests burn.
To the south, rain blows,
waters rise. Coming soon
to a neighborhood near you,
hail of bullets,
mushroom cloud.

I'm not sure
who's in charge here.
All I know:
I am worn with trying
to siphon truth
from air and airwaves,
misleading leaders,
wars of words.
All is not well.
We soldier on.

Sisyphus in Autumn 🍂

for Jeff

Dry leaves layer the lawn,
scuttle in the wind,
like crabs across the concrete.
The rain decoupages them
into slick patterns on the driveway.

Because he treasures his acre of suburbia,
he labors for hours to uncover
the smooth carpet of dim grass,
clear the ragged piles from the sidewalk.
It looks really nice now, I tell him, as he hangs
the blower on a hook in the carport, removes
the protective earphones from his head.
But even as I say this, I can see over his shoulder—
a few leaves stealing back onto their property,
as if the trees were dropping crisp handkerchiefs,
sending brown-paper missives slowly down to earth.

In a few days, he will begin again.

On the Brink 🐦

I would swear this is where Christ
spent his forty days and nights,
parched, starved, on the brink.

What tempts me as I stand here,
something like hunger
gnawing my long bones?
I have tried turning stones into bread,
and though the urge to jump lurks,
I will not do it.

I am drawn to descend, walk down
into the sheer silence, become
a speck moving between
sunbaked rocks and hard places,
toward a remnant river.

I want to know what would find me first:
rattlesnake or ranger,
heatstroke or angel,
fiend, god.

This Lonely Cognizance 🐦

He has hiked deep into the woods
and told himself he will not leave
until he has his answer,
and on that first night
he cannot sleep for listening—
the insects, the stirrings
in the dry leaves, the yowl of the coyote.
One snap of one twig
and he almost shouts: *Who's there?*
At first light he shuts his eyes
and when he wakes mid-morning
vows to keep a fire burning
through the sullen night,
spends the afternoon gathering
downed branches, broken limbs.
When darkness returns, he is ready,
has layered his wood pile properly,
strikes a match on the sole of his boot.
He places potatoes on the fire,
sets an open can of soup at the edge.
His thoughts turn to the Lakota,
their sweat lodges, the desire he feels
for revelation, a splintering of the self
into these billion stars, reassembly
as a better man, transfused, refined,
steady as this great gray mountain.
As the night deepens, he adds wood
to the fire, lets the smoke saturate
his hair, lungs, dizzying him until
the crack and pop of the ashing logs
rouse his heart, incite a vision:

a solitary man beside a campfire,
face illumined by orange glow,
viewed from a great distance,
seeing himself, being seen
watched over, watching,
acknowledged surely,
and he thinks this is his answer,
this seeing and being seen,
this knowing, which seems enough.
In the morning
he will pack his few things

Waiting for a Pear to Ripen in Pittsburgh 🖎

My first trip to the city with the stolid name, steely past, I
arrive dulled, heavy-laden. At the hotel conference center,
the wait staff sets a bowl of fruit on the table. I take a firm
green pear to my room in hopes it will ripen by week's end.

I did not imagine this would be Pittsburgh: three eloquent
rivers rimmed with wooded hills, crossed with yellow
bridges. After sunset, wild geese fly black and noisy against
remnant light.

I could be a different person if there were always rivers
flowing outside my window—and I only had to cross
the street at dusk to walk their banks. The moon throws
its light on the Allegheny just before the confluence, a
shimmering foil for the stadium's gaudy glow. The breeze
whiffs of oak leaves.

For six restive nights, alone in my hotel room, I've gazed
out at these rivers, waited for something to loosen. This last
morning, the pear, blushed and golden, yields to my touch.

Lament for the Doused Campfire

Farewell to crackle and warmth,
the pop and tumble of logs,
orange tongues
that dance and leap,
won't let you look away.

>An arc of creek water streams
>from the green bucket.
>Elongated hiss,
>tang of sodden ash.
>Muttering embers.
>Darkness.

Consolation for your fresh grief:
the stridulations
of a thousand crickets.
In the cold distance,
a coyote clears his throat.
The Milky Way spills
across the blackboard sky.

Rite of Passage on Red Top Mountain

for Ben

Somewhere along the trail my son has passed me and now
I am following him. His muscling calves disappear around
a bend. A few minutes later he calls to me—*Mama? Coming*,
I say. He waits until I'm in sight to turn back to the path.
Half a mile more, all birdsong ceases. There's a man just
inside the woods, a sullen stag dressed in a sleeveless
T-shirt and dirty jeans, arms covered in crude tattoos. He
glares at me but does not speak. Heart races; legs will not. I
catch a glimpse of my son standing a few yards up the path.
Come on, Mom, he says in a doughty voice. When I catch up
to him, he puts one arm around my waist, shows me the
pocketknife in his other hand. We don't look back.

A Cup of Grace 🖋

Imagine a cup of grace
poured into your palm,
which is also cupped.
What will you do
with this unwarranted bounty?

Rub it over your face,
a holy moisturizer?
Drink it, in desperate gulps or
measured sips? Shape it
into a ball of cloud,
then hand it over
to the old woman, the sick
child, the lost man?

Convert yourself
into an instrument of grace.
A piccolo perhaps, viola, or timpani,
like a heartbeat, an unforsaken
heartbeat.

Imagine a symphony as you pray,
consider the notes you would play.
Then go in grace.
Uncup your hand.

Sweater Weather

Disrobing trees, woolly clouds.
A thin creek stitches itself
into the red valley.
You want to be warmer.
A skein of geese pulls
across the afternoon sky.

January's Hair 🕊

is gray and thin, frizzes over the river,
tangles in the bare trees.
She places a hex over the land,
cloaks it in slush and ice, renders
it colorless. Her bitter breath
withers the grass, stiffens
the birds on their roosts. And yet,
I owe her. She keeps me inside
a calescent tower, frequently gifts me
a slim slant of sunlight, heightens
my senses by banishing the frivolous,
calls me to let down my hair.

Narrow Escape

Languor of lingerie, parsing of pearls,
whistle and whir of the wind.

A tapering of the long road before you,
crush of the sky round the bend.

Forsake threadbare paths, the furrows
of protocol, sorrow of window and pane.

Pinpoint the hour you seek to dismantle,
the lair of your life in the rain.

Grit of the pear on the tip of your tongue,
scintilla of smoke in your hair.

Sensation of strength, premonition of mercy,
a descant of steps on the stair.

Pawn your blue velvet cloak.
Disappear into the trees.

The Only Child Lies Awake
during a Windstorm

listening to pecans thud on the silver roof.
Hers is the back bedroom that faces the yard.
She wonders if a limb from the old tree
might crash into the room, imagines herself
smashed in bed, splintered wood raining everywhere—
her body littered with cracked nuts,
hair full of torn leaves. She doesn't think it fair
her parents have each other in the front bedroom
while she must sleep alone, but she is
too frightened to go to them.

Her father is a deep sleeper; her mother is not.
She often senses her mother wandering
through the dark house like a ghost. Tonight,
as the storm moans, the ghost walks into her room
in an aqua nightgown. The only child slides out
from under the covers, puts her arms
around the ghost's neck, is carried into her parents'
warm bed where she will soon fall asleep,
her father's rhythmic snores foiling
the fitful, immoderate wind.

Running through Greenhouses 🖊

Our family friends owned a nursery,
warren of glass-paned greenhouses
built by the German great-grandfather.
Humid kingdom through which we ran.

We hid and sought among geraniums,
chrysanthemums, the beginnings of
poinsettias, stalks of Easter lily,
fat hydrangea. Celadon lizards scurried
among the terra cotta pots, pulsed
their rosy dewlaps.

Sometimes we'd encounter the father
tending the plants. He'd growl at us
to make us squeal, send us running
to the next sweaty greenhouse, this one
incubating white azaleas.

Overhead misters hissed, glided
up and down the rows, reviving
the thick scent of black soil dotted
with fertilizer, fecundity nestling
in our clothes and hair until we smelled
like all the other growing things.

Ottoman Feast 🐦

A luncheon of honey and walnuts
is all I have time for today, thick tablespoon
of sweet amber on a stoneware dish,
into which I dip the wrinkled nuts.
It's Turkish honey, the label informs,
produced by bees foraging nectar from Rock Rose,
Citrus, Wildflowers & Turkish pines.

O Trader Joe's, I thank you—for elevating my mood
with your enticing description. Honeybees of Turkey,
you have my gratitude—for pollinating a place
I yearn to see. O Rock Rose, you Mediterranean beauty,
O treacly pine, bless you for making my humble lunch
so much more than it might have been.

Interior Scene with Family and Small Bird 🐦

Once when you and your brother were small,
we filled a plastic feeder with sweet red water.
I climbed the stepladder, hung it
outside the dining room window.

You weren't sure you'd seen a hummingbird before,
so your brother described one to you:
How tiny it was, how quick. How its wings
beat so fast, they disappeared.

We were vigilant at mealtimes, looked up at every bite.
Then one supper, after we'd said grace and you were
telling your dad about your day—the books you'd brought home
from the preschool library, the classroom hedgehog—
it appeared, fairy-like, treading air beside the feeder.

You sucked in your breath;
the four of us exchanged sideways glances.
Everybody freeze, I whispered,
laying one finger across my lips.
But of course, we didn't.

Dogwood Winter 🖋

Three days after Easter,
and the temperature
has slipped, fallen.

Flakes of flowering cherry
swirl with pale petals
of unseasonable snow.

A bald yellow egg
from the weekend's hunt
lies unfound on the bitter ground.

We pull our sweaters
tight around us, hope
the hyacinths won't freeze, wait

for spring to strong-arm winter,
roll it back
where it belongs.

In the DuPont Forest 🦢

for Lynn

Light striped the pliant trail.
The woods exhaled an incense
of moss and mold, newborn and old,
carpet of leaves and custodial trees
muffling the way until
we came to the place
where the water fell,
white and lavish,
to thunderous applause.
It was my birthday.

Downing the Sun 🖎

In the west now, a searing sunset
illumines the imprint of your breast on mine.

There have you traveled on purpose without me,
no forwarding address, no departing line.

Is this the glimmer for which you betrayed me?
Can you remember the slant of our sky?

Walking as straight as your tall boots will let you,
shed shards of moonrise, a husked lullaby.

I have been cauterized, left in the shadows,
longing for glimpses of walnuts and gorse.

If I sing softly, will dragonflies nestle me,
grant me sweet amnesty from this remorse?

I don a crown of mountaintops, leap heavily
into the evening sea, still do not drown.

Bones to Pick ❦

The old couple picks at the day
as if it were a roasted chicken.
They dine on the breast at breakfast,
devour the liver, heart, and gizzard at lunch,
are down to the dark meat for dinner.
Then the real gnawing begins.
They pull the last shreds of meat from the ribs,
pry the morsels from the wings. One of them
wrests the wishbone from the greasy carcass
and holds it aloft. She wants to paint it gold
and hang it on a ribbon, but he calls for the question,
there and then. *What's your wish?* he demands,
Pick a side and pull. And so, with a crack of the cartilage,
it is decided: Which one of them
will turn in for the evening, which one
will sit alone in the dark.

Whole, Wide World 🖋

Heat rises from asphalt in corrugations;
flecks of rainbow snag the skeins
of oscillating sprinklers. Unseen bird
in the palmetto next door
repeats a two-beat trill
punctual as a heartbeat.

Vacant seashell cupped to the ear
will surely sound like a faraway ocean.
Fragrant earth beneath the feet
undulates, emits a fulsome vibrato.

Everything aquiver, everything wavering—
this waterfall world inclines
so voluptuously toward the light.

Still 🕊

for my father

Spring arrives early where we come from,
on the fat-oaked, moss-draped coast.
At your burial in late February, the azaleas
were already blooming, sand gnats circling
in the warm Geechee air. I was hot
with grief and anger; your winter
had come too soon.

In the eighteen years since, you have sent:
one spectacular rainbow arching over the marsh,
a soft and unexpected snowfall, a lone heron
watching from a drought-drained pond.

I want to tell you that spring
has come early again this year.
Bulbs have burst through the ground
to scent this place; palmettos clatter
in the breeze. Though I have learned
to bury anger, in this warmed soil,
my grief blooms still.

Graveyard

The summer grass is sown with bones:
dinosaurs and giant sloths;
Choctaw and Cherokee;
slain Civil War soldiers.

Loyal dogs are buried in backyards,
unfaithful cats go missing. Milk cows
lie down in green pastures;
black bears fall to the forest floor.

Mixed among them: my father's bones,
spotted and cracked with cancer;
my grandmother, bled dry
after the birth of my mother;
a fragmented cousin returned
in a body bag from Viet Nam.

The facts are nonnegotiable.
Even if you mean no harm,
a gritty wind blows over the earth,
raps and riddles your shoulders.

The half-moon is a headstone lodged
in the infinite throat of the night.

Landscape with River Birch 🐛

There is no river here,
just a gunite swimming pool.
You were planted for your bark,
crispy curls of taupe, cinnamon, cream.
But you grew too tall, forked over the roof,
cast the climbing roses into shade.

He resolved to remove your offending limb,
stanch the shower of leaves
that threatened to clog the gutter,
allow more sun to fall
on his odorless buds.

I bought him a book about pruning,
told him it mattered how and when
a tree was cut. He didn't need a book,
was mad to use his ladder and saw,
wouldn't wait for summer
when your sap would slow.
He pulled the saw teeth back and forth
until he severed one of your arms.

The pruning book warned
that river birches are *bleeders*,
shouldn't be cut in spring
when their juices freely flow. For days

you've been weeping without ceasing,
sap pooling on the driveway, a little lake.
The drops spatter when they land.

I stand in the drip,
look up at your wound,
let the tears fall on my face.

After the Blight 🕊

after Anya Silver

The poem was the wood and the way out of the wood.
The poet wound her way through a forest,
up to the porch of an old cabin, its floor planked
with chestnut cut and planed before the blight,
back when the trees cast shady alcoves,
sheltered songbirds. (Remember the smell
of roasting chestnuts?) She napped on the porch,
on the smooth planks, rose to gather fresh words,
plucked them from the limbs of the ghost trees,
lined up the words, sent the poem downstream,
out of the wood and into the field,
which was full of light.

Back to the River 🐦

Everywhere I look
there is work to be done:
the feeding of the poor,
the rescue of damaged children,
a need to understand
the diminishment of the aged.
There are also the dishes,
smeared with remnants of rich stew,
clumps of yellow day lilies
in want of division,
windowpanes perpetually smudged
because a resolute cardinal
keeps pecking to come in.
When I walk
along the Chattahoochee,
I note with envy the grace
of the great blue heron,
which opens its wide wings
and sails across the water,
steps delicately along the bank,
always seems to know
which way to turn.

The Poet at Fifty-Nine

after Larry Levis

Autumn is a glum raisin,
plumped with sweet wine,
stirred into a spiced batter.
As the cake bakes, scents rising,
I think of the woman
who taught me to make it,
of everything I learned
from all the old women:
How to seed zinnias and play canasta,
make artichoke relish and ambrosia,
tie French knots, polish the silver,
the hemming and pressing of skirts.

These women spun stories
on the porch in evening,
waiting for the house to cool.
Hung strips of foil on grapevines
so blue jays wouldn't steal the ripe fruit.
Snatched clothes off lines before storms struck,
wrote letters to men at war. They learned to swim
through green creeks of disappointment
and some spoke softly of babies they'd lost.

The first dark has entered the trees,
diminishing their saffron glow.
I've mixed a cocktail, opened a can of almonds
to eat with the warm cake. My thoughts meld
with the murmurings of the old women,
in the dim parlors of memory.
The words go on, a braided rope.
Lessons have been learned.
The grapevines are bare.
The land is mine.

The Poetry Reading 🖋

The young male poets read their work
and it's all about dangerous things:
bloody fights with brothers, dumpster diving,
freight-train jumping, construction-site theft.
They're slim and attractive, and the audience
gasps at their insouciance, their derring-do.
They are busy living borderless lives,
starring in movie-poems.

If you are a female poet past middle age,
and a mother to boot, you will feel hopelessly dull
as you listen to them, ashamed of your rule-following,
your quiet poems about a pair of deer at twilight,
the vulnerable nape of your small son's neck.
In your next life you swear you'll be a man,
do shocking things and then write about them,
sip whiskey as you read aloud.

Then you remember the infants at your breast,
how important you felt as you fed them,
how they cried for you—and only you— in the night.
You are not sorry, most of the time, that you picked
the dinner table life, wrote about walking the flat trails
along the river, the lacy ferns and upright herons,
even if it meant you were destined to bore young gods
with your quotidian body of work.

How Much I Love You All

The rain came down
thick and gray this morning.
I counted the wrecks I passed
on the interstate, grateful
I wasn't one of them
then thought how it might be
to lie on the knife-cold pavement
bleeding out in the January rain—
sirens wailing, strangers bending over—
and when I did, I realized
how much I love you all,
every last, warm one of you,
the timbre of your voices,
the verity in your eyes.
Love enough to make a body rise
and beg another chance.

Acknowledgements

I want to thank the editors and staff of the following journals for publishing my work:

Amethyst Review: "The Shoal Lilies" and "A Cup of Grace"

Appalachian Heritage (now Appalachian Review): "Luna Moth"; "The Poet at Fifty-Nine"; "After the Blight"; and "The Last Wild Passenger Pigeon Makes Her Concession Speech"

Boston Literary Review: "Old Beach House" (formerly "Haunted House")

Cider Press Review: "Downing the Sun"

Curio Poetry: "Sisyphus in Autumn"

Deep South Magazine: "Running through Greenhouses" and "On the Chestatee, Late September"

Flycatcher: "On the Brink" and "Trespass"

Foundling Review: "Eggshell"

Gravel: "The Only Child Lies Awake during a Windstorm"

Heron Tree: "Order *Lepidoptera*, Family *Papilionoidea*"

James Dickey Review: "This Lonely Cognizance"

Loose Change Magazine: "Whereupon the Writer Thinks She Is the Center of the Universe" and "Bones to Pick"

Main Street Rag: "A Story of the Earth" and "Distant Shore"

Menacing Hedge: "Narrow Escape"

Muddy River Poetry Review: "Raven, in the Back of Beyond"

San Pedro River Review: "Bliss"

Slice of Life: "Back to the River"

Split Rock Review: "Autobiography"

Southern Humanities Review: "Graveyard"

Southern Poetry Review: "Childhood, Heavy with Hydrangea"

Still: The Journal: "Fluent in Rivers"; "Sweater Weather"; "The (Barely) Bearable Heaviness of Being—Fall 2017"; "Waiting for a Pear to Ripen in Pittsburgh"; "July's Thick Kingdom"; and "And So, September"

Tar River Poetry: "Parched" and "Ottoman Feast"

Terratory Journal: "Encounter in a Dry Riverbed"; "Above All Else"; and "By June the Light Begins to Breathe"

The Christian Century: "Petrichor"

The Southern Women's Review: "Dogwood Winter" and "Interior Scene with Family and Small Bird"

The Sunlight Review: "In the DuPont Forest"; "Waxing Poetic"; and "Invasive Species"

Turtle Island Quarterly: "Lowcountry River"

Valparaiso Poetry Review: "Sapelo"

Verse-Virtual: "Rite of Passage on Red Top Mountain"

Yemassee: "The Husker"

Deep appreciation also goes to my mentor William Wright, and to Christopher Martin, Cecilia Woloch, Ralph Wilson, the late Susan Laughter Meyers, and Diane Kistner (FutureCycle Press) for helping me develop as a poet. I thank Wright's Writers and the Side Door Poets (Karen Paul Holmes at the helm, Maggie, Trish, Rupert, Dan, Jesse, Sally, Diana, Ricks, Jane, Andrea & Georgia) for their deft suggestions and poetic friendship.

Sandy Spencer Coomer and the Rockvale Writers Colony gave me the peace and quiet I needed to finish this manuscript. Multi-talented publisher Christine Brooks Cote brought the book to life at Shanti Arts. And I'll ever and always be grateful for the love and encouragement of Jeff, Ben, and Rosalee Lewis (who is also a great editor and designer), my supportive girlfriends, and my lovely parents, Norma and Lee Brewin. There is no me without all of you.

About the Author

KATHLEEN BREWIN LEWIS grew up among the moss-draped oaks of Savannah, Georgia, eighteen miles from the Atlantic Ocean, in a land crossed with creeks and rivers. A graduate of Wake Forest University, she received a master of arts in professional writing, with a concentration in creative writing, from Kennesaw State University. Although she now lives in the bustling city of Atlanta, she is grateful to be just minutes from the walking trails beside the Chattahoochee River and from the roads that lead to timbered hikes in the north Georgia and North Carolina mountains. She and her husband, Jeff, have two grown children, Ben and Rosalee. A Georgia Master Naturalist, Kathleen is the author of two chapbooks of poetry, *Fluent in Rivers* and *July's Thick Kingdom*. *Magicicada & Other Marvels* is her first full-length collection.

Printed in the USA
CPSIA information can be obtained
at www.ICGtesting.com
LVHW041536191124
797070LV00030B/399